Thinking Stories 1

Thinking Stories 1

Philosophical Inquiry for Children

Edited by Philip Cam

Illustrations by Ken Rinkel

Acknowledgement is made to the following journals in which earlier versions of some of the stories first appeared: *Analytic Teaching, Thinking: The Journal of Philosophy for Children*, and the *Bulletin of the International Council for Philosophical Inquiry with Children*.

10 9 8 7 6

Cover illustration and book design by
Karen Rinkel
One Plus One Design Pty Ltd
PO Box 517, Narrabeen, NSW

Printed and bound by
Southwood Press
(02) 9560 5100
www.southwoodpress.com.au

For the Publisher
Hale & Iremonger Pty Limited
PO Box 205, Alexandria, NSW 2015
www.haleiremonger.com

National Library of Australia Cataloguing-in-publication entry
Thinking stories. 1, philosophical inquiry for children.

ISBN 0 86806 482 3

1. Children's stories. 2. Philosophy – Study and teaching (Primary)
I. Cam, Philip, 1948–   II. Rinkel, Ken. (Series: Children's philosophy series; 1).

808.89282

Contents

Introduction,
or Making a Beginning

PHILIP CAM

Thank goodness. I thought for a moment that you weren't going to read this introduction. Then I wouldn't get to talk to you, and tell you all about this book.

This is a special book. It's a book of thinking stories. 5
What's a thinking story? Let's see. You could say that fairytales are fanciful. Fables have morals. Ghost stories are spooky. Mystery stories have hidden endings. So thinking stories are . . .

'Oh, no! You're not going to tell them, are you? 10
They are supposed to figure things like that out for themselves.'

That's Ann. I just knew that she wouldn't be able to keep quiet long enough for me to have my say. Ann is one of our authors. 'Ann, do you have to interrupt me as 15
soon as I start talking to the children about this book?'

'I couldn't stop myself. It's the way that you began. You told me that the children were going to do the talking. They were going to talk about what interested them. And they were going to figure things 20
out for themselves. So you can't have an introduction

in which you do all the talking, and tell everyone what's what. Besides, how do you expect me to keep quiet for so long, when you put my stories right at the end of the book?'

5   *Excuse me just a moment everyone.* 'Ann, I was just about to explain those things to the children. Now I'll have to figure out how to explain them all over again. In any case, who's the only person with two stories in this book? And are they *both* at the end? No,

10   they're not. You couldn't have two stories that are both at the end of a book, anyway. Only the *last* story can be at *the end.*'

'Really? I don't see why you can't talk about more than one story being at the end of a book. Otherwise

15   you might just as well say that the end of a book is only the book's last page, or just the last words — where it says *The End.* I know, why don't we ask the children what they think?'

'Ann, would you cut that out! Here I am trying to

20   tell the children what this book is about, and you're leading us right off track. Would you mind letting me get on with it?' *Good. Now everyone, as I was saying . . .*

'Excuse me!'

'What's the problem now, Ann?'

25   'Mat's here. I think he wants to say something.'

Ann is talking about Matthew. He's another one of the authors. Please excuse me once again. This will only

take a moment. 'Hello, Mat! Did you want to say something?'

'Hi, Phil. Yes, I just wanted to say that I think Ann's right. I mean, why don't you ask the children whether they would like to discuss that question about whether there can be two stories at the end of a book? They might also like to talk about what they think makes something a thinking story. Better still, they may like to raise some questions of their own.'

'But Mat, I was going to explain to the children how we will be discussing all kinds of things that the stories make them wonder about. Everyone will be able to ask questions about the things that they find interesting. We will put all the questions on the board, and then we will talk about them together.'

'Phil! Phil! Phil!'

'Yes, Ann?'

'Were you also going to tell the children about how they will need to listen carefully to one another? How it's all right to disagree with someone, but that you might need to give a reason for what you say? After all, what's better: to disagree with each other without knowing why, or to try to work out *why* we disagree?'

'Thank you, Ann. I was going to tell the children all about that too. Thinking about reasons is important. It helps you to understand things.'

'And when you listen to the reasons that other

people give, it helps you to understand *them*. What do you think of that, Phil?'

'I guess you're right, Ann. Perhaps we could say that, in this way, we come to see other people's points of view. So even though we don't always agree, we can come to understand each other better.'

'Right.'

'Do you know what I am thinking, Ann? I'm thinking that all this thinking that the children and I will be doing together is going to be fun. I can't wait for us to start reading the stories.'

'Phil, there's something that it seems I need to explain.'

'What's that, Ann?'

'You're not going to be reading the stories with the children.'

'I'm not?'

'No, you're not.'

'That's not fair. I mean, I didn't realise that I would just produce this book and, well, that would be that. But now I come to think about it, I suppose that I am not going to get to say anything else after I've finished this introduction.'

'Poor Phil. I'll tell you what.'

'What?'

'While we have been talking, the other authors have all been listening, and they have come up with lots of things that they would like to talk about. Steven wants to know what makes a story a *thinking* story. And Yeh has asked what makes a question interesting. (Now that's an interesting question!) Ron has a question about when it's all right to interrupt someone and when it's not all right. Phil has a question too. (No, Phil. Not you. I mean that the *other* Phil has a question.) He wants to know how important it is to be able to ask good questions. Is it as important as being able to give good answers? Gilbert's question is about whether you can listen and think at the same time. Oh yes, and Mat has a question. He wants to know what are all the other things that we do when we reason together, besides giving reasons. (That sounds like a hard question.) Oh yes! I have a question too. Does every thinking story have a story about how it came to be made up? Mat has written all the questions on the board, and now the authors are ready for the discussion to begin. Why don't you join us? It would be just like old times.'

'What a wonderful invitation! Thank you, Ann. I can't wait.'

'Just before we go, Phil, aren't you forgetting something?'

'Oh dear! Am I? What is it?'

'You haven't said good-bye to the children.'

'Oh, my goodness! How thoughtless I am. I almost forgot that they were here. They've been so quiet. I'll just say good-bye.'

Thanks for listening, everyone. I hope that you get as much enjoyment from reading these stories, and discussing your ideas, as I got from producing this book. Farewell! I mean, good luck with the thinking! 5

Your
Place or Mine?

STEVEN BEAR

Otto lived in a cave that was very near some bushes on which grew the most delicious berries. There were trees and flowers, and a lot of other animals and birds. There was also a stream near the cave where Otto lived, and that was where he met Una.

Una lived in the stream, together with plants and other fish, and bugs, and snakes. Sometimes animals would come to drink, or cool off, or find tasty things to eat. That's what Otto was doing there on the afternoon that he met Una. He was trying to catch something good to eat. Otto was a bear.

In fact, when he saw Una for the first time, swimming along in the effortless way that Una swims, Otto almost ate her. Otto's only thought was, *That fish looks delicious, and I'm so hungry.*

Just as Una was about to swim past, and Otto was raising his big front paw with its long, sharp front claws, Una looked up and saw him. For some reason, instead of thinking, *Oh no, a bear, I must swim away as fast as I can,* Una thought, *Hello! Who is this big, beautiful creature? I will talk to him!*

She popped her head out of the stream and said, 'Hello. I am Una, who are you?' Otto stood there with his right front paw raised over the water, and he couldn't believe his furry bear ears. He just stood there on three legs and said, 'Uhhhhhhh!'

Una dipped gracefully back in the water, then poked her head out again and said, 'What did you say your name was?'

'Otto,' said the bear, very slowly. And then he added 'Uhhhhhhh!' once again.

Una dipped under the surface of the water again, reappeared, and said 'Hello Otto. What does "Uhhhhhhh" mean?'

When Una tried to imitate the way Otto said 'Uhhhhhhh' it sounded funny, because Otto's voice was a deep, booming bear growl, and Una's voice was high and soft. Otto smiled and said, 'Una?'

After another dip in the stream, Una said, 'It's a beautiful day.'

'Yes . . . Una.'

When Otto said her name, Una had to laugh because Otto's way of saying it was so different from her own. When Una laughed, her whole body shook back and forth in the water a little, and it sent soft ripples rolling out to the edge of the stream.

By now, Otto had forgotten that he had wanted to eat Una for lunch. He had lowered his paw and sat down in the middle of the stream. And Una, who seemed a bit exhausted by all this peeping out of the
5   stream and talking, started to swim around Otto, going in slow, graceful circles. Otto watched, and thought to himself, *She is beautiful.*

After a short while, Una popped her head out of the stream and said, 'I've got to go now, Otto. Can you
10   come back tomorrow?'

'Uhhhhh, OK,' growled Otto.

Una laughed and said, 'Bye, Otto,' and swam off downstream.

Otto just sat there for a minute, then got to his
15   feet and walked out of the stream towards his cave. *I'll eat some berries for lunch today,* he thought to himself as he walked home. *I'm not so hungry anyway.*

✳ ✳ ✳

Otto had never been spoken to by a fish before. He knew how good they tasted, but he had never noticed
20   how interesting and pretty a fish could be before that afternoon. Otto thought about Una quite a bit before he returned to the stream the next day and waited for her to appear. Before long, there she was.

'Hello Otto,' she said, as she poked her head out of
25   the stream, her tail working all the time to support

herself. Otto greeted his new friend in his friendliest
bear tone of voice. Then Una slid back under water and
began to swim around Otto, first in simple circles, and
then in a pattern that looked like this:

And before long she was swimming around the   5
bear in a way that looked like this:

Otto laughed and clapped his big front paws
together. Una raised her head above the water and
smiled. The two friends were each glad that the other
was having a good time. Otto tilted his head up to the   10
sky and half-sang, half-growled, a song like one he
had heard some of the other bears of the wood sing.

This is how it went:

GGGRROOWWOOOOO

GGGRROOWWOOOOO

Snort Snort

5   GGGRROOWWOOOOO

Una listened to Otto's song and danced to it under the water in a way that was both strong and graceful. She felt the vibrations of Otto's booming voice in the water, and danced to the song as though she had been

10 doing it all her life. *No bear has ever sung to me like this before. No fish, either,* thought Una, as she danced around Otto, sometimes swimming so close that his fur touched her smooth scales.

Otto sang his bear song, and Una danced her fish

15 dance, and the two of them went on like this for a good long time. Then Una popped her head out of the stream, looked at Otto, and the two of them laughed and laughed, until they were both quite tired.

'Will you come back tomorrow, Otto?'

20 'Yes, Una. Grroowww.'

'Bye, Otto.'

'Bye, Una,' said Otto, sitting there looking down at the fish with a big bear smile on his face.

After a moment, Una turned to swim away

25 downstream, where the water gets quite deep, but then she turned back. 'Otto,' she said, 'would you like to come downstream with me tomorrow, and see where I

make my home? The water here is very shallow for me.
'I would like that,' said Otto. 'And the next day you
might like to visit my home,' he added. 'It's beautiful. I
think you will love it.'

'All right,' said Una. 'Shall I meet you here 5
tomorrow?'

Otto growled in agreement.

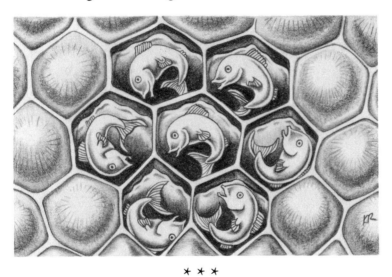

* * *

The following afternoon, as agreed, the two friends met
at their usual place. 10

'Ready Otto?'

'Yes,' growled Otto, who was a little afraid, but
didn't want to show it.

'This way, come on,' said Una, as she began
swimming slowly downstream. Off they went together. 15

Before long the water was up to Otto's chin. He
stopped.

19

'Come on Otto, it's very beautiful further downstream.' Otto took a deep bear breath and went forward until he was completely under water.

It's dark and mysterious, thought Otto, *and*
5   *exciting.* Yet, in almost no time, the bear needed more air to breathe, and there wasn't any. Una was playfully swimming around Otto and leading him into even deeper water, but Otto turned around and struggled back towards the shallow water as fast as he could go —
10   which wasn't very fast. Then he bounced through the shallows all the way back to their usual meeting place, and sat down in the middle of the stream to catch his breath. He felt rather glum.

Una swam back to her big, furry friend and said,
15   'You don't like my part of the stream, do you, Otto?' She was no longer in her usual, happy mood.

'It's beautiful,' replied Otto, 'but I need to breathe air, and I can't in the part of the stream where you live.'

'Oh,' said Una, thoughtfully.

20   'But you may like the cave that I live in very much,' Otto said hopefully.

'I would like to see your home,' said Una, trying to hide her disappointment at the day's misadventure.

'Shall we meet again tomorrow?' asked Otto.

25   'All right,' said Una. 'Bye, Otto.'

'Bye, Una.'

✳ ✳ ✳

That afternoon and evening Otto prepared his cave so it would be beautiful for Una. He gathered flowers and berries and put them in the cave, and cleaned up his bear messes wherever he could.

5 When he met Una the next day, Otto's fur was very clean and smooth. 'Are you ready?' he asked.

'Yes, Otto. How do we get to your cave?'

'I'll put you in my mouth and we'll walk there.'

'Otto!' said Una in a shocked voice.

10 'Don't worry,' said Otto, 'You'll be safe.'

Una trusted Otto, so when he put his mouth down to the surface of the water, Una swam in so that her head stuck out of the left side of Otto's mouth, and her tail stuck out of the right side. 'OK,' said Una

15 bravely, when she was as comfortable as she was going to get.

Otto lifted his head out of the stream and quickly began walking towards the cave, which was not far away.

20 Una's first thought was how bright and colourful everything was. Yet in just a few moments she began to choke and feel dizzy. 'Take me back, Otto!' she gasped. 'Take me back now.'

'Gggrrgghh uunnngguurrnnggh,' said Otto. He

25 had meant to say, 'You haven't seen my home yet,' but couldn't speak clearly with a gasping, thrashing fish in his mouth.

'Otto! Water! Help!' said Una, who had never felt worse in her life. Otto dashed back to the stream and gently placed Una back in the shallow water. In a couple of minutes, Una was able to swim normally and speak again.   5

'Oh, Otto,' she said. 'I've got to go now.'

'Bye, Una,' said Otto, his voice now soft and sad.

Una looked up at the bear in silence for a moment, then she slipped back under the water and headed downstream. For quite a while, Otto sat still in   10 the water, silently watching the stream flow by, and then he headed home.

⋆ ⋆ ⋆

For the next few days, Una stayed in the deep water and Otto stayed in his cave, except when he needed some berries. It was about a week later that Otto and Una met   15 again in the shallow part of the stream. Otto was fishing.

'Otto!' cried Una. Then she swam up and said in her most serious fish voice, 'Otto . . . I belong in the deep water with my friends.'   20

'And I should spend more time eating,' Otto responded. 'Cold weather is coming and I have to get fat for winter. I sleep through the winter and I have to stay warm. I'm trying to catch some lunch right now.'

'Otto!'   25

'Well, I've had a lot to eat here, I think I'll go home now,' Otto said, and he turned and started towards the grassy ground on the bank of the stream. As he put one paw on the ground, he heard the familiar, soft voice.

'Otto.'

Otto turned his head towards the middle of the stream, but kept his paw on the grass. Una's little head looked as tiny as could be from the bank.

'We can still be friends until the winter, can't we, Otto?'

'Yes, Una,' Otto said, one paw still on the warm grass.

'See you soon, Otto,' Una said in a trying-to-be-cheerful fish tone of voice.

'See you soon, Una,' Otto called back. Then he pulled himself out of the water and continued his walk home.

The
Bird's Nest

YEH HSENG-HONG

*J*en-Jen came back from school. The minute she saw her mother she cried, 'Mummy, what happened to your hair?'

Her mother said, 'How do you like it? Isn't it beautiful? I've just had a permanent.' Jen-Jen puckered her lip. She circled around her mother. 'Not very good-looking. I don't like it. I liked it the way it was. It looks so fuzzy now and it seems to have grown bigger. It looks like a *bird's nest.*'

Jen-Jen's mother tried to comfort her, and seemingly to comfort herself. 'Oh, Jen-Jen! I can see why you don't like my hair now. But maybe after a few days you'll get used to it. Then you'll start to like it.'

Jen-Jen didn't seem to agree. 'Maybe. But I still feel that your head is twice as big as yesterday — and it's growing like a huge bird's nest.'

First thing the next morning, Jen-Jen's mother got up and looked in the mirror. 'My God!' she exclaimed. After a night's sleep her hair was worse than yesterday. She combed it for a long time and started to blow it with a hair dryer. She took a shower, came out into the

bedroom, combed it again, and blew it again and again. Her hair got bigger and bigger. Jen-Jen's mother looked sad and then angry. She thought about the money she had spent on the permanent. She didn't know what to do with her hair now. 5

Jen-Jen walked in. She was startled and screamed, 'Mummy, your bird's nest is growing. You told me it was going to be better, but it's worse.'

Her mother answered, 'Grrrl! Don't say that anymore. I know it's ugly.' 10

But Jen-Jen would not give up. 'Why did you have a permanent, Mummy? Your hair was so straight and good-looking. Now it's ugly. It looks like a bird's nest.'

'Bird's nest! Bird's nest!' her mother cried. 'How many times are you going to say it? Please cut it out. 15 Okay?'

Jen-Jen just stood there and said calmly, 'It's a fact, isn't it, Mummy? It's a bird's nest.'

Her mother's temper rose like a thirty-foot fire and she screamed, 'I begged you not to say that again. 20 And you said it. I don't want to talk about my hair any more.'

Jen-Jen was silent for a long time. Then she opened her mouth. 'Remember last year when I was playing the piano? You used to stand by me and kept 25 saying that my playing was not right. I was sad and angry. I wanted you to go away. But you wouldn't listen.

I already knew that I needed to practise much more. I was practising *then*. But you kept on nagging all the time.'

Jen-Jen's mother seemed very surprised. But she said nothing. Then, in a hard tone of voice, grinding her teeth, she said, 'Hair and piano are two different things. Don't get them mixed up.'

'Are they really different?' Jen-Jen responded mildly. 'I thought they were the same. What *is* the difference?'

Tommy and
the Time Turtle

MATTHEW LIPMAN

B-*r-r-r-ing!*

Tommy picked up the telephone. 'Hello,' he said, in a small voice.

The voice on the other end of the telephone said, 'Hello! This is your *chance of a lifetime!* All I want you to do is give me a *minute!'*

The person calling spoke so slowly that Tommy thought, *You've already taken a minute!* But aloud he said, 'I'll go get my father. Who should I say is calling?'

'I,' said the caller, 'am the *Time Turtle. Don't* get your father! I want to talk to *you!* All I want you to do is give me a *minute* of your *time!'*

Tommy frowned and thought, *That makes* two *minutes!* But now Tommy was interested. He asked, 'You're collecting time?'

'Of *course!'* the Time Turtle replied. 'I'm so *slow,* I need all of it I can get!' Then he added, 'Bless my ears, boy, you do ask a lot of questions!'

'I'm afraid I don't have much to give you,' said Tommy, who was now beginning to feel a bit sorry for the Time Turtle.

'That's *quite* all *right!*' the Time Turtle drawled. 'I'm not asking you to give me some of your time as a *gift!* I will give you something *in return* for it: *the chance of a lifetime!* Would you like *that?*'

5 'Oh, very much!' Tommy exclaimed. 'How do you want me to give you my time?'

'You've already *done* it,' said the Time Turtle, with a chuckle. 'So now you are entitled to a *ticket.* Tell me your *name* and I'll put it on a ticket. Then I'll put your

10 ticket in this big *bowl* with all these other tickets, and when the winning ticket is drawn, we'll see if you've *won.* So what's your name?'

'Tommy.' Since the Time Turtle didn't reply, Tommy added, 'T-O-M-M-Y.'

15 'Thank you!' said the Time Turtle. 'I was never very good in *spelling!*'

Tommy thought, *So what* was *he good in?* But he was too polite to ask.

'I'll write your name on this ticket with the

20 number 95748 on it. Here we go: T...U...M...M...Y.'

Tommy said sharply, 'No, no, that's not right! Not Tummy: *Tommy!*'

'Oh, oh, excuse me,' said the Time Turtle, sounding really sorry. 'But now I've fixed it. *T-O-M-M-Y.*

25 Is that right?'

'Yes,' Tommy answered. 'So now, when will you pick the winning ticket?'

'Why, right now, of course!' responded the Time Turtle. 'First I shake up all the tickets in the bowl, like this, then I fish around, and then I pick one out! And the name on the winning ticket is — the name on the winning ticket is —'

'Yes, yes, tell me,' Tommy said breathlessly.

'I need to get my *glasses.* Where did I *leave* them? On, *here* they are! The name on the winning ticket is *Tommy!* Oh, my, aren't *you* the lucky one! You get a *ticket* and immediately you're a *winner!*'

Tommy was thrilled and said so. 'I've never won anything before, in my whole *life!*' he told the turtle. 'Wait 'til I tell my family.' But then he realised something. 'But-but-you didn't tell me — *what* did I *win?*'

The Time Turtle replied, 'You're absolutely *right.* I *did* forget! Bless my suspenders!' And he laughed to himself for so long that he forgot to tell Tommy *again* what he had won.

Tommy cleared his throat politely and said, 'So I won —'

'You won *time,* of course,' said the Time Turtle. 'Everyone puts a little time *in* and someone takes it all *out.* Bless my toenails, aren't *you* the lucky one!'

'I don't understand,' said Tommy. 'My ticket won. Or I won. Whatever. But what? I can't wait to find out!'

'And you have a right to know, my boy, you have a

right to know!' laughed the Time Turtle. 'Bless my belly-button —'

Tommy interrupted, a bit impatiently, 'I didn't think — well, you know, I didn't think turtles *had* belly buttons — '

'What I meant to say was, bless my kidleys,' said the Time Turtle.

'Don't you mean *kidneys?*' asked Tommy, beginning to be a bit annoyed.

'That's what I said, didle I?' responded the Time Turtle.

Tommy just raised his eyebrows. He remarked, 'I'm still waiting to find out what I won.'

'Oh, bless my socks,' exclaimed the Time Turtle, 'of course, of course! What you *won!* Why, you can now make a wish!'

'For what?' Tommy asked, bewildered.

'Well, you have all that time you've won, so now you must figure out how to use it.'

'Like *how?*' Tommy demanded, frowning at the telephone.

The Time Turtle sighed. 'Bless my walkman! Think, boy, think! Use your head! What would you like that takes too much time?'

Tommy replied, 'I don't have to think. I already know the answer to that one. For my birthday, last week, I asked for a tree by my window, and my parents gave me a tiny tree that hardly reaches as high as my belt. I'm afraid I looked disappointed. They asked me what was wrong, and I said that it would take many years, because trees grow very slowly. And I said I didn't

5   want a tree that grew slowly; I needed one that would grow sky-high overnight.'

'So wish for it,' said the Time Turtle. 'If you need to get back to me, my 'phone number is 107-249-4630.' With that he hung up.

10   Tommy quickly wrote the number on the back of his hand, in case he should forget it. Then he made his wish.

The next morning, the moment after he woke up, Tommy rushed to his window. Sure enough, a great tree

15   was pressing against the window panes, and Tommy could not see out.

He hurried downstairs and outside. Alongside the house was a tree as tall as a great skyscraper! Its top was lost in the clouds! The Time Turtle had made good on

20   his promise!

Tommy walked all around the base of the tree, and then went off a way and stared at the tremendous height of it. Then he ran back inside the house, going first to the bathroom to brush his teeth.

25   As he was brushing his teeth, he happened to look at himself in the mirror over the sink.

Only, it wasn't himself he saw in the mirror! It was

someone else — an old man!

What had happened? Tommy was so frightened, he could hardly breathe.

The Time Turtle's number was still on his hand! He rushed to the telephone and dialled 107-249-4630. It $\quad$ 5 seemed to take forever, but finally he heard a recorded

message: 'The number you have dialled is not in service. For further assistance, dial 800-TURTLE.'

Tommy dialled 800-TURTLE. To his relief, the Time Turtle answered. Tommy told the Time Turtle $\quad$ 10 what had happened. He ended by saying, 'The tree is very nice. But when I look in the mirror, I see an old man. Who's he?'

'Who's he?' exclaimed the Time Turtle. 'Why, bless my knee-caps, boy, he's *you*, that's who he is! Of course, $\quad$ 15 it's an older you than you were yesterday!'

'But I don't understand,' wailed Tommy. 'I

thought you would just make *the tree* grow older, *not me too!*'

The Time Turtle said softly, 'I'm so sorry, Tommy. I thought you understood. I can only do what I can do. I can make time go fast forward, but it has to be *for everything,* not just for one thing at a time. I thought you understood that when you made your wish.'

Tommy was outraged. 'What do you mean, you thought I understood it? I didn't understand anything of the kind! Now you've turned me into an old man.' Tommy brushed away angry tears with the back of his hand. 'Do you think that's what I would have chosen if I had known?'

The voice of the Time Turtle was even softer now, almost a whisper. 'Would you like to go back to the way you were?'

Tommy leapt at the chance. 'Could I? Do you mean it?'

The Time Turtle chuckled. '*No problem!* Bless my spectacles, no problem at all!'

In practically no time at all, Tommy felt a shiver run through his whole body, from his scalp down to the soles of his feet. He ran to the bathroom and looked in the mirror. He looked the same as he had yesterday!

He ran outside. There was the little tree, sticking just above the ground, underneath the window to his room.

Tommy ran back to the room and picked up the 'phone. The Time Turtle must have hung up.

Tommy dialled again and again, but there was no answer at 800-TURTLE. It wasn't as if there was a recorded message saying that the number was out of service or disconnected. There was just no answer.

Then Tommy remembered — the number on the back of his hand! But it was just a blur.

All of this happened some years ago, but it's still very fresh in Tommy's mind. And every year, on his birthday, he tries dialling 800-TURTLE. He no longer expects to hear the Time Turtle's comfortable drawl, but he dials the number anyhow, hoping that it might once again be so.

A Night
Under the Stars

ANN MARGARET SHARP

Not long ago, I learned about death. Til then I hadn't thought about it.

My father's father who lived with us died. He was my grandfather. He was also my close friend. I loved him very much. One day he was here and the next day he wasn't. I felt like I had a big hole in my chest.

I would come home from school and talk to my grandfather. He was always willing to listen. He would pay close attention to what I would say. His questions always showed that he thought what I said was worthwhile. I had the feeling that he was thinking about every word that would come out of my mouth. He never interrupted me. I liked that.

One evening before he died, he said to me, 'Brendan, how about a walk?'

'I'd like to sleep out under the stars, Grandpa. It's warm this evening. You could tell me about the Southern Cross and the Evening Star again. Then we could find Orion. What do you think?'

'I'll go and pack some things,' he said.

When we got to the beach, we chose a spot

protected by the rocks. My grandfather gathered some small pieces of wood that were lying in the sand and he made a fire. The fire against the ocean smelled great. The sound of the waves crashing against the rocks mixed with the crackling of the kindling and the breeze 5 of the night air. I felt good.

'Grandpa, tell me a story.'

Grandpa didn't say anything for a long time. He just looked out to the ocean. I was beginning to think he was never going to speak when he said, 'I knew a 10 man for a long time. He was my friend. His name was Juan Carlos. He had left his home town when he was a young man. He just walked away from his father, his mother, his home, everything. He even left his job. He lived in our village for many years after that. Then, one 15 day, the police came and took him away. I didn't see him again. Many years later I heard that he had died. I felt very alone.'

My grandfather took a stick and started to poke at the fire to make it more fierce. I couldn't help staring at the red and orange sparks as they rose to the sky.

'What happened then, Grandpa?'

'Years later, I was riding my horse through the mountains in northern Spain and something very strange happened. A storm came up right as dark was coming on. It began to snow very hard. I was afraid I wouldn't make it to the next town. Then, in the distance, I saw my friend's face. It was formed in stone. His profile was there, in stone, straight ahead of me.'

Grandfather paused, staring into the embers. He added, softly, 'Now, changed into stone, my friend lives forever.'

'That's a very spooky story,' I said.

'Why do you say that?' my grandfather asked.

'I'm not sure. It gives me goosebumps. But I like the idea of your friend living forever, Grandpa.'

'Me too, Brendan. Me too!'

That was the last talk I had with my grandfather. Remember what I told you before. One day he was here and the next day he wasn't.

I still find it hard to believe.

The
Knife

PHILIP GUIN

*C*arl never planned to steal the knife. He'd gone to Beecham's Hardware first thing in the morning to buy a can of paint, in order to touch up the boards of his tree house. But the colour he wanted was in the storage room, and as Mr. Beecham went to fetch it, leaving him alone in the store, Carl's attention strayed to the merchandise displays.

Because it was so early, no one besides Carl was in the store. He liked being alone with all the new things, gleaming fishing poles, handsome flashlights and transistors. Then he noticed the usually locked case containing the expensive hunting knives.

The case was open! Carl examined an attractive knife and thought how useful it would be in working around his tree house. *What luck,* he said to himself, *it could be days before anyone realises there's a knife missing, and by then who could accuse me?* Carl slipped the knife into the deep pocket of his winter jacket. When Mr. Beecham returned with the can of paint, Carl quickly paid the bill and left the store.

Once out of the store, Carl raced away, exhilarated
by his bold adventure, but nonetheless anxious that he
might have been found out. As he rounded the corner,
he unexpectedly collided with his friend Pete. Both boys
went sprawling on the pavement. Luckily, neither was   5
injured, and having regained his breath, Carl excitedly

bragged to his friend about his deed. As the boys talked,
Carl noticed that Pete had misgivings. Carl was
annoyed.

'I don't care what you say, if you can get away with   10
it, what difference does it make?' Carl looked
admiringly at the knife he'd taken from the hardware
store. Pete, obviously upset by his friend's story, tried to
persuade him to return the knife.

'Look,' Pete cautioned, 'you could still be caught.   15
Like you said, you were the only one in the store, and
that knife is worth a lot of money — they're going to

miss it and when they put two and two together, they're going to be on top of you in no time. Maybe you could just take it back and put it where you got it.'

'No way,' Carl objected, 'they've no proof, and 5 besides you're the only one I've told. Since you're my best friend, you can't turn me in. So it's their word against mine, and I'm not about to admit anything. Sometimes you have to lie to save yourself — it's as simple as that. Maybe you're just jealous because I got 10 away with it.'

Just then Raphael ambled by. 'What's going on you guys?' he asked cheerfully. Both boys were extremely agitated by now, and though Raphael was a classmate, they didn't feel they wanted to tell him what 15 had happened. Pete said that they were just talking about stealing and whether it's okay to steal if you can get away with it. Raphael listened attentively to his friends: Carl arguing that it's okay, so long as you don't get caught; and Pete countering that you shouldn't 20 because you could get caught.

When he had the chance, Raphael broke in. 'But it's against the law to steal whether you get caught or not. We have to obey the law, don't we?'

'Laws are made to be broken,' Carl snapped 25 contemptuously, 'and if you can get away with breaking the law, who's the wiser? Anyhow, people are always breaking the law, speeding on highways, cheating on

bus fares, shoplifting — the only thing that counts is whether you get caught.'

'But they do get caught and how do you know you won't?' Pete put in quietly.

5   Carl became cocky. 'It's just like cheating in a test. If you're clever, the odds are that you won't get caught, and if you're careful when you take something like a knife, the odds are that you'll get away with it — otherwise, forget it.'

10   The boys walked on down the street still vigorously examining the pros and cons of stealing. Soon they met Shirley and Glenda on their way to the pharmacy. The boys hurriedly filled the girls in on the discussion, but continued to talk among themselves. Finally, Raphael
15   asked the girls for their opinions.

When the boys had calmed down, Shirley hesitantly offered, 'Even though you might not get caught, and even though there might not be any laws against it, stealing could still be wrong.'

20   The boys demanded to know how that could be. 'Well,' Shirley began, 'what if everyone went around stealing, what then? No one could trust anyone; only the very strongest could survive in such a world. So, if you're going to steal, you better be sure you're the
25   strongest.'

The boys remained silent.

'What if you just don't like stealing,' questioned

Glenda, 'would the consequences make any difference to whether you thought it was alright? Besides, even though I knew I'd never get caught, and even though stealing wasn't against the law, I'd never steal just because to *me* it's wrong.' Glenda then added, 'And I 5 don't think I'd want a thief for a friend.'

By this time Carl was looking disturbed. He mumbled an excuse and left his friends still arguing. Out of sight, Carl ran on in the direction of Beecham's Hardware. He thought of his friends, especially of 10 Glenda, of his fondness for her, of how she always seemed interested in his ideas and made him feel comfortable. To lose her friendship would be disastrous. When he reached Beecham's, he mounted the steps two at a time, but entered the store quietly. As 15 before, no one, including Mr. Beecham, was in sight. Carl made his way to the case containing the hunting knives. He dug into his pocket and felt the knife at the same instant that he felt a hand on his shoulder.

'What have you there, Carl?' Mr. Beecham asked. 20

'I just couldn't keep it, Mr. Beecham,' Carl blurted out as he handed the knife to the tall burly man. 'My friends convinced me it's wrong to steal.'

As Mr. Beecham listened, Carl recounted the details of taking the knife and of his subsequent 25 discussion with his friends. He didn't, however, tell of his feelings for Glenda. When Carl had finished, his

head hung down and tears were uncontrollably filling his eyes and running down his cheeks. Mr. Beecham searched a long time for words. Just as Carl was convinced there was about to be a 'phone call to the
5 police, Mr. Beecham spoke.

'You know what I think?'

'No, Mr. Beecham.'

'It sounds to me like you have some pretty smart friends.'

10 'I know.'

'Well, what do you think should happen now?'

'I don't know, but I guess I'll have to pay for what I've done. Will I have to go to jail?'

'I'm not so sure you'd pay for it *just* by going to
15 jail,' Mr. Beecham said evenly. Carl wondered what Mr. Beecham could possibly mean; he was terrified that the very worst was about to happen.

'Tell you what. Come on down here to the store for the next three Saturdays and help me out. If you do
20 that, the knife is yours. You'll have paid for it.'

Relieved and grateful, Carl vigorously shook his head up and down indicating 'yes', then quickly left the store. As before, when he had departed Beecham's with the knife, Carl felt exhilarated; but now, somehow, the
25 feeling was different. He knew he had a lot to think about.

Linda
and Clara

RON REED

*L*inda is tall, very tall. Today she bumped her head on the awning of Oscar's Delicatessen. This was the first time that ever happened. She ran into the store, hoping that Oscar had lowered his awning. Alas, it was at the same level it had been for years. Linda concluded that, although she was tall, very tall, she was still growing.

She slouched out the door, trying to look short. It did not work. She just looked like a tall person slouching, trying to look short. She turned a corner and bumped into her best friend, Clara.

Clara was downcast. The skin around her eyes looked puffy. Her nose was red.

Now, there are some people who cry very easily. Indeed, Linda is such a person. Linda cries at sad movies and during sad television shows. Sometimes she even cries over television commercials. But Clara is not that sort of person, even though she is Linda's best friend. Clara never cries. Well, almost never.

Linda looked down at her friend. Clara looked up at hers. Then Clara did something that caught Linda by surprise. She kicked Linda in the shin.

* * *

Linda limped down Stirling Street. Her leg hurt, but not nearly as much as her feelings. She was tall, very tall. 5
Soon, she feared, she would be too tall. And even worse, she had no one to confide in. Unless, of course, you counted Clara. But Linda did not want to count Clara. You could not count on a person who went around kicking you in the shin. 10

She checked out her reflection in the window of the Little Miss Fashion Store. She cringed. She could not see the top of her head. Her reflection grew past the frame of the window. The world was becoming too small for her reflection. And for her. 15

She climbed the stairs to her apartment. She remembered when she had to struggle to climb the stairs. She had to lift her legs as high as they would go to get from one step to the next. But now she did not have that problem. She took two steps at a time. Then 20
she took three steps at a time. When she made it to four at a time, she began to cry.

She opened the door to her apartment. Her

mother and father were sitting in the kitchen, chatting over coffee. She looked at them and exclaimed, 'You always say that everything is going to be all right. That makes me mad, so mad!' She ran into her bedroom and

5 slammed the door.

* * *

The next day, Linda saw Clara walking to school. Linda thought about hiding in the church on the corner. Her leg still hurt.

Clara saw her friend and ran to her. She

10 apologised to Linda. 'I'm sorry. Everybody was making fun of me for being short. And then I saw you, and you looked so beautiful. So tall, so very tall. And I got mad and kicked you. And I'm sorry.'

Linda did not believe her friend. Well, she did

15 believe that Clara was sorry. She just did not believe her

when she said that Linda was beautiful. She was just very tall.

Linda said, 'But *you're* the beautiful one.' Clara was petite and pretty. Clara did not believe Linda either, but she was glad that they were still friends.   5

★ ★ ★

Clara and Linda are walking down Stirling Street. Linda is on the outside, near the curb, trying to look as short as she possibly can. Clara walks on the inside, and stands as straight as she can. Yet they are happy walking together.   10

The
Echo Sisters

GILBERT TALBOT

It all started on a Sunday morning, two years ago. I remember, because I was six and now I'm eight. There were big black clouds rolling across the sky. I wanted to play indoors with my
5 friends, but my dad had another idea.

'Come on, Marie-Neige,' he said, 'let's take a ride!'

'Where are we going, Daddy?'

'We're going to Alma for a big outdoor demonstration.'

10 I didn't know what a demonstration was, so I didn't want to go.

'No,' I said, 'I want to stay here and play with my friends.'

'In Alma, you will find a lot of new friends to play
15 with you. We will sing and dance together and play all kinds of games.'

I was not really fond of singing and dancing in the rain, but a car ride could be fun after all. If only ...

'May I invite a friend to come with me?' I asked.

20 'Sure. Why not? But first ask her parents.'

I phoned Lola. She's my friend. But Lola's parents

did not agree and I had to go alone. So I took Aggie, my big lamb, and held her tight against my chest. I fell asleep on the back seat, listening to the song of the rain on the roof of the car. When I woke up, we were in a place I had never been before. 5

'Where are we, Daddy?' I asked, still half-asleep.

'We're at Alma, Sleeping Beauty,' he said gently.

Since the rain had stopped for a moment, we got out of the car, holding hands, and headed towards a row of tables where some people were waiting. 10

'Do we register here?' my dad asked a nice man standing behind a table.

'You can register at any of the tables,' the man answered. 'Just choose the letter you prefer and then go with the other people over there. They will tell you what 15 to do.'

I know which letter I prefer now — it's 'U' — but at that time I was not even sure what letters there were. Did you know all the letters of the alphabet when you where six? Even my dad had to ask for a letter. Can you 20 imagine?

'Can we be part of your letter?' he asked a lady at another table.

'Sorry, we're full,' she answered. 'But I think that the third "A" has some more room. Hurry up, though. 25 It will soon begin.'

I couldn't understand what was going on.

'Why the third "A", Daddy?'

'Because there are three "A"s in the word A-shu-A-pmushu-A-n.'

'What's *Mouchouane?*'

5   'The Ashuapmushuan, Marie-Neige, is a very powerful river which your father and your godfather tried to canoe down once!'

'Why do we have to go in an "A"?'

'You see all those people over there? We will join

10   them to write in big, big letters the word

A-S-H-U-A-P-M-U-S-H-U-A-N

so that it can be seen from the air.'

'But I don't know how to write,' I objected. 'I don't want to go there.'

15   'You don't have to know how to write, Marie-Neige. You will be in a letter with some other people, and everybody will sing and dance together. We'll all have a lot of fun. You'll see.'

The rain started to fall again. A loudspeaker

20   announced, 'Don't worry everyone. The rain will soon stop, and then the helicopter will be able to rise.'

Dad had brought some of those ugly green garbage bags. He made one hole in the bottom for the head and one on each side for the arms. 'There you go,'

25   he said with a big smile, 'a brand new rain coat for Marie-Neige.'

He also made me a rain cap. I didn't like either the cap or the coat. They made me look like a clown! How would you like to be dressed in garbage bags? I'm not garbage!

While they were waiting for the rain to stop, people were rehearsing jumps, waves and dances, so that later they could be seen from the air.

'Come on Marie-Neige. Jump with us. It's fun!'

'I want to go home. I'm cold. I'm hungry.'

I started to cry, but the loudspeaker broke in to announce that the helicopter had finally risen. We had to follow our group leaders now: marching first, then running barefooted in the wet grass, shouting and singing loud enough for the film crew to hear and see everybody from up there. I was pulled up and pushed down by the people's waves. It was no fun at all! Everybody tried to cheer me up, but nothing helped. I got out of the letter just when people started shouting *'Save the Ashuapmushuan! Save our river!'*

This really puzzled me. So I came right back in to ask, 'Why do we have to save the river, Dad?'

'Because the Hydro Power Company wants to build some dams which will destroy the *ecosystems* that depend on the river.'

'Are you kidding?' I laughed. 'Who are the *echo sisters?*'

'Not the echo sisters, dummy! *Ecosystems.*'

Then he started to give me a long explanation that I never understood. Finally, he said that an ecosystem was a kind of puzzle. So, I was twice as puzzled. Do you know how bad it can be when you don't understand
5 something and the more people try to explain the more you get confused? So I started to cry again. My father looked at the sky, rolling his eyes and raising his hands up as if he wanted to clutch at a cloud.

An Indian girl who was in the same letter as ours,
10 came up to me and said, 'I heard your name "Marie-Neige" which means "snow", and you know what? My name is Yih Sheue. It means *"gentle snow flake"*. Isn't it strange? We come from different places, we don't know each other and here we are together trying to save the
15 same river.'

She seemed so nice. But was she really? How could I know? I decided that I would ask her about why we must save the river.

'It's not just the river,' she said. 'If they build dams
20 on the Ashuapmushuan, it will flood all the animal's homes along the river.'

'Oh, I see! I sure don't want that to happen. Why didn't you tell me that before, Dad?'

'It's not only the animals who will lose their
25 homes,' said my father. 'All the plants and trees along the river will disappear under water, if the Power Company builds the dams. You see, the trees, plants and

animals can't protest. That's why we must do it for them.'

After some reflection, I said, 'But what about you "snowflakes", don't your people kill animals? I have seen Indians hunting and killing buffaloes on T.V.'

'You can't believe everything that's on T.V.,' she

answered. But after some hesitation, she added, 'You're right, though, Marie-Neige. We kill animals for eating and making clothes, but we never destroy an animal species like the white people are doing now. My people, The Montagnais, live along the Ashuapmushuan River and want to protect their native land and all the plants and animals that live there.'

We fell silent for a while. I was trying to figure out what Yih Sheue had said. I did not agree with her people killing the animals, but since she wanted to protect the animals' homes, and since the animals are my friends, I decided that she could be my friend too. So I decided to join in with her and my dad in the singing and dancing.

5 'Save the Mouchouane!' I shouted. 'Save the house of the animals!'

* * *

After the demonstration, we all went to a stadium, where some films were shown. The loudspeaker announced that the videotape taken from the helicopter would be shown on television. I was excited. 'Is it true, 10 Daddy? Will we be on television?'

'Yes, Marie-Neige, we will be on the news tonight!'

Usually I hate the news. Dad usually wants to watch it and I have to miss my favourite program. But if we are going to be on, that's different! 'The news is not 15 so dull after all,' I admitted.

'Shhh,' said somebody behind us. 'The show is about to start.'

They showed us a movie about the Ashuapmushuan. We followed a wild river, as if we 20 were birds flying over it. It gathered between towering mountains, rushed over grand rapids and falls, and flowed down through dark forests. Other rivers joined it along the way. We heard about the pike and salmon swimming in its water. We saw bears fishing on its 25 shore. There were beavers building dams, moose having their bath and all kinds of birds flying by. I was so impressed, I could not take my eyes from the screen. I just couldn't understand why people would want to destroy such a beautiful place.

At the end, I asked my father, 'Why does the High   5
Pro Company want to destroy that river, Daddy?'

'Because the Hydro Company wants more *power,*' he said. 'But if there are enough of us to oppose it, then the Company will have to give up its project.'

I wanted to know more, but a guy behind us   10
yelled at my father, 'You make the Hydro Power Company sound like a monster, who wants to destroy everything.' Then the man took me by the shoulder and said, 'Somebody has to tell you the truth, young lady. I work for the Hydro Power Company and I can tell you   15
that we take care of the animals before building a dam.'

I couldn't say a word. I was frightened.

'Do you know what electricity is?' he went on.

Of course I know what electricity is, I thought to myself. 'Electricity is what you get inside of lamps when   20
they're on,' I told him.

'Right,' he said. 'And it's what makes the washing machine work and the television and all the electrical appliances in your house. You see, we need more and more electricity to make better homes and provide   25
better living for everybody. That's why we have to build new dams. Otherwise we would have to use nuclear

energy, or keep on using coal to produce electricity. Maybe you don't know it, but the burning of coal also produces the greenhouse effect. Did your father tell you about that?'

'My dad never told me anything about green houses,' I said, 'but my uncle, who's a farmer, has got one. It is a place made of plastic windows, where they grow vegetables and flowers.'

Dad started laughing, but not the man, who told me very seriously, 'You're right, little girl. But if we keep on burning coal to produce electricity, the whole planet will become a greenhouse. Have you ever noticed how hot it is inside your uncle's greenhouse?'

'Yes, I remember. It's so warm and damp, even when it's snowing outside. I'd like to live in a green house.'

'But, if we lived in a greenhouse, my girl, the snow and ice would melt, the North Pole would turn into water, and the whole world would be flooded, not just the animals' homes in this valley.'

That really frightened me. 'Dad, is it true? Will we all be flooded? I won't drown, will I? Because I know how to swim.'

Before dad could say a word, the man butted in, 'Maybe you won't drown, but your house will be flooded, and all the houses of your friends, and maybe your friends themselves will drown. Who knows what could happen? So you see, we are flooding just a few animal homes in order to save our own.'

'But you told me that you take care of the animals before you build your dam!'

'Some of them, sure! We'll move them to the zoo, where they will have some brand-new homes. And you know, the Hydro Power Company will pay for all the expenses!'

I wanted to know more about that zoo, but the loudspeaker broke in. 'Ladies and gentlemen, I have the pleasure to inform you that there were more than one thousand five hundred people at the demonstration. You can count them for yourself on the screen now.'

I couldn't count the people. I didn't know how to at that time, and anyhow, there were far too many of them. Besides, sometimes the image was upside down, or we just saw the clouds, or we couldn't see anything at all. I was kind of dizzy, just as if I were on a roller-coaster.

'Daddy,' I asked, 'Why is it that when things are far away, we don't see them anymore?'

'Because we have to be close to see a thing well,' he answered, putting his glasses on the tip of his nose.

'Yeah, but Daddy, when things are close, we don't see them too well either.'

'It's true, my baby, we have to be at the right distance.'

Suddenly he jumped with excitement. 'Look, Marie-Neige! There we are on the screen!'

'But I can't see myself,' I cried.

'Of course you can't, because you are too little.'

'But how come we can see the letters and not the people?' 5

'Because the letters are much bigger, silly! We are just like the little pieces of the puzzle forming the letters. And the letters put together form the word

"A S H U A P M U S H U A N".' 10

Here was that puzzle again. 'The letters are like the echo sisters, then?' I asked.

'You're right,' he said. 'I never thought of it that way. In a way we can say that we formed an *ecosystem of letters*.' 15

Right at that moment, a question that I had in my mind for a long time came right into my mouth. 'Daddy?'

'Yes, Marie-Neige.'

'Why do letters form words?' I knew it was a 20 difficult question, because it took a while for my dad to find the answer. And when he finally did answer, he talked like my teacher.

'You see, Marie-Neige, letters alone can't form words. They are sad because they have no friends to talk 25 to. But when they form words, they are happy because now they are together.'

My dad seemed happy with that answer, but I wasn't satisfied, because what he said reminded me of another question I often thought about. You know how it is, don't you? One question raises another and you never know where it will finally lead.

'Daddy?'

'Yes, Marie-Neige?'

'When you read me a story, there are lots of words. Are the stories also *echo sisters?*'

'Yes, I suppose that stories are also ecosystems,' he said. 'Some of them are even *about* ecosystems,' he added with a laugh.

That was really interesting. I knew what I wanted to ask him right away. 'OK, *Papa,*' I said. (That's what I call him when I want something very important.) 'Tonight will you read me the story of the *echo sisters?*'

'Oh no, Marie-Neige. I have to clean the house tonight. It's a real mess! Especially in your room, you little witch!'

I didn't add one word. I just stood there in silence.

Finally he said, 'Alright, Marie-Neige, I'll read you the story, but I will have to write it first. First I'll write the story, and then I promise that I will read it to you.'

Oh, how I love my dad! I know him so well. It's always like that with him. At first he says no. Then he becomes silent. Then he always says yes. Is it the same with all parents?

Back home, he sat in front of his computer and took the rest of the day to write our story. And that night he read it to me, when I went to bed. I listened very carefully and corrected him when he went wrong. After the fourth reading, I finally fell asleep and dreamt of the *echo sisters* living happily along the Mouchouane River. 5

* * *

I have always remembered that story. But I'm afraid that I will forget it when I grow up. That's why I wanted to share it with you. Did you like it? 10

Gabriel's Story

ANN MARGARET SHARP

I am finally getting round to writing my story. Early this school year, I had a problem, a real problem. For our language lessons, we had to write stories. I didn't know how to write stories. I was a failure. Do you know what it is to be failing at school? Do you know how it feels? I'm a person who likes to succeed, and when I don't I feel very badly about myself.

When I began the year, I enjoyed reading the stories in our textbook. But when Mrs. Laverty said, 'If you want to pass this year, make up your mind that you will write many short stories,' my heart sank. I felt miserable. I knew I could never write a story of my own. The more stories I read, the more I told myself, *never, never, never.*

At the beginning of the fourth lesson, Mrs. Laverty announced that we would have to hand in one short story every two weeks, in addition to our other work. For my first story, I wrote one paragraph about my dog, Rory. I said he is big and friendly and eats a lot of food very quickly. Then I said I've never seen a dog eat a meal so fast. That's all I wrote.

When Mrs. Laverty returned the story to me, I was shocked. My story had failed. And at the top of the paper, in big red handwriting, she had written, 'Gabriel, this is not a story. The work is unsatisfactory.' 5

Reading these words, I got up out of my desk and walked from the classroom in a daze. Luckily, the bell had just rung. I didn't even hear it. Nor did I notice Heidi come up by my side to take my arm. 'What's the matter, Gabriel?' 10

'Heidi,' I said, 'I'll never pass. I can't even tell what makes a story a story. I'm going to flunk, for sure.' Heidi's my best friend and I was sure she would understand my despair. She knows I like to do well at school. Sometimes she teases me by saying, 'Gabriel, 15 don't think so well of yourself.'

But now she seemed very caring. 'You won't flunk. Don't even think that, Gabriel. It would be terrible, just terrible, if you didn't come with us to the high school.' The idea of not going to high school with my classmates 20 next year was so horrible that I would feel nauseous every time the thought came into my mind. I spent most of my time trying not to think about the whole situation. Yet, I knew for sure that everyone was required to pass in their language studies before they 25 could go on to the high school.

There were times when I was tempted to tell Mrs.

Laverty, 'Look, I don't know what a short story is and even if I did know, I wouldn't be able to write one. I can write essays, I can do the exercises in grammar, and I can write good letters. I can even write poems. But I just can't write stories.'

I never voiced these thoughts to Mrs. Laverty.

Maybe I was afraid, or ashamed. Maybe I thought that she would think I was just making up excuses. So instead of saying something, I just continued to hand in failing stories, or attempts at stories, while at the same time feeling worse and worse about myself.

Talk about low self-esteem. I lost my appetite. Most afternoons, I didn't feel like playing ball or going swimming or riding my bicycle. I didn't even want to talk to Heidi on the 'phone. If I looked at television, I wasn't able to concentrate enough to follow the simplest plot. It was as if my mind were dead. Hour after hour, I would sit and mope. Finally, my mother said to me, 'Gabriel, how about taking a few days off from school and going to see your grandmother? It might be just the kind of change you need.'

My grandmother lived about a two hours' drive   5 away from our home. I always thought of her as a very good friend. She seemed always to want the best for me, and always thought I could do anything I really wanted to do. Now I wished I could be as sure of myself as Grandma was. Nearly every year, as school holidays   10 drew near, she would invite me to stay with her for a few days. I looked forward to these visits. In the summer, we would walk and talk together, pick and press flowers, and bake many kinds of delicious cakes and cookies in her oven. In the winter, there was usually   15 a fire burning and wonderful smells of cinnamon and herbs would fill the room. Her home was very special.

My grandmother loved animals. She had a big dog named Castle and two cats, Mieke and Clio, who would play with the dog and chase birds all day. Outside four   20 of her windows, my grandmother had hung large bird feeders and would delight in telling me about the many birds who came to eat in her garden. Some would eat the sunflower seeds, while others would eat the mixture that she made up herself in the garage. I never knew   25 anyone who knew more about birds than my grandmother.

'How are things going in school, Gabriel?'

'Not very well, Grandma,' I said. 'We have to write short stories and I can't figure out what makes a piece of writing a short story. Everything I've turned in has been failing. I'm about to give up.'

'Don't do that, Gabriel. You know I have a lot of faith in you. Your grandfather used to say that there are many ways to plant a garden. I'm sure you'll find a way. I can remember when I was in school, I was doing poorly in history. We had a large textbook and I couldn't understand it. I was failing one test after another. My teacher might have known a lot about history, but he knew very little about teaching. He would speak very quickly, while we were supposed to take notes. I could never get the listening, the writing, and the understanding to work together.'

'What did you do?'

'My mother suggested that I go to the library and ask the librarian if he had any books dealing with the period we were studying. I found many books that I could understand. They were written by people who presented history as an adventure story. I discovered myself reading these stories with pleasure before I would go to sleep each night. During the year, I must have read two dozen of them.'

'Did you pass the subject?'

'Not only did I pass, but I got a very good grade.

That grade meant more to me than all the other grades that year. It were as if I had discovered something very important about school and myself at the same time.'

'You didn't give up,' I said slowly while looking out the window at three little scarlet-bellied robins grouped on the bird feeder.

'No, I didn't give up. I found another way to get the job done. I bet if we give it some thought, we can come up with a way for you to learn how to write short stories.'

'I hope so, Grandma. The first thing we have to do is figure out what makes a piece of writing a short story,' I said gloomily. 'There must be some rules.'

'I don't know about rules, Gabriel,' Grandma said in a low tone. 'Perhaps criteria are what you are after,' she muttered, as if she were speaking to herself. 'But stop worrying. We'll figure it out. Now, why don't we go into the kitchen and have some blueberry muffins and hot chocolate.'

Sitting at Grandma's table, I began to feel better. I liked being there with her. Grandma always had a special way of helping me to feel good about myself again when things are going wrong. I looked around the room and thought to myself, *This is a great room.* The dark windows framed the fields outside while admitting a soft light into the room. It were as if the large wooden table and cabinets glowed from within, creating a space

where I could finally feel safe. Mieke and Clio came over and rubbed against my legs for a while, and finally settled down to nap under the kitchen table.

After I had gobbled down three blueberry muffins and two cups of hot chocolate, I said, 'Grandma, I'd like to be able to do more than just write a passing story. I'd like to be able to produce a *good* story.'

'That's a wise distinction, Gabriel,' Grandma said, sitting down next to me and smoothing her apron over and over again. 'Maybe it has something to do with character.'

When Grandma said this, I didn't think she was making any sense. What did character have to do with writing a good story? I noticed that I felt quite annoyed and said to myself, '*Character*', *that's one of those suspicious words I often hear adults using, but never know quite how they are using it.*

'Grandma, what are you talking about? I'm not interested in what makes a person good. I want to create a good piece of work. I don't even know what you mean by the word "character".' Boy, did I sound irritated. I even shocked myself.

Grandma eyed me intently. 'Well, Gabriel, I think character is an important thing to consider when judging a piece of work — or a person, for that matter — but it's the hardest thing to explain.'

'That's not much help, Grandma. Don't be

mysterious with me, please. I couldn't take that right now.'

Grandma got up, walked around the kitchen and then sat down at the kitchen table again. She thought for a long while, fingering a wisp of her curly grey hair and looking through the doorway into the living room. I couldn't help but notice that even though her skin was quite wrinkled, it still looked very soft and clear. Finally, she said slowly, 'I wish I could be clearer. I have a hunch that anything I say will be problematic. I've never found talking about things like this very easy.'

At that point, I felt a little guilty. *Why was I so annoyed?* I said to myself. *She was trying to help. I can be so mean at times.*

'Gabriel, when I use the word "character," I mean a certain habitual way of behaving, an aiming or striving for wholeness or seamlessness in what we choose to do. A piece of work has character when every piece fits together and makes up a certain unity or harmony. In a short story, it is not a matter of how many words, but the quality of the experience we are trying to communicate, and how we connect the words we choose to convey this experience.'

I felt as if a big hole had come into my stomach as I listened to Grandma's words. I just knew I didn't understand what she was talking about. She must have sensed how I felt, because she paused for a while and looked at me very carefully. She poured me some more hot chocolate from her old white china coffee pot and went on. 'It's like dressmaking,' she said. 'One is not interested in how much cloth one has, but in the quality of the cloth, and the appropriateness of the pattern one has chosen. Good dressmaking depends on what we do with the cloth, how we change it into something that appears almost seamless, balanced and whole. Now, does that help any?'

'I'm afraid not, Grandma. I don't know anything about dressmaking.'

'Dressmaking is only an analogy, Gabriel. Look, when someone chooses to write something good, she goes about developing certain skills, procedures, habits that stand her in good stead with each and every piece of writing. Even if she revises these skills and habits over and over again, she tries to keep a sense of the whole. It's this sense of the whole that dictates what words one should use and how one should proceed.'

'Oh,' I said. I sensed that Grandma was getting tired and I was becoming restless. But Grandma continued, 'You know, Gabriel, one important skill for the short story writer is learning to pay close attention to daily experience — imagining the story in the many things that we do, the story behind the many things that happen to us. Everything has a story. Sometimes I think that even the words we use to describe what happens to us have a story, just waiting to be told.'

I thought about this for a while and said, 'Oh, like wondering what might be the story of the new blue jay who came to your feeder this morning.'

5   'That's a good example, Gabriel. I bet you could write a fine story about my new blue jay, where he might have come from, what he left behind, what has happened to him on his many flights, and why he has decided to settle around my house this winter. Just

10   think of the time he will have protecting himself from Mieke and Clio. At least I make sure those cats wear bells on their collars to warn they are near.'

All this happened one month before my grandmother died. I still remember all the details about

15   my visit to her farmhouse. The cupcakes and cookies that came out of her oven were so delicious, light and sweet that we quickly ate nearly everything we baked. The old pressed flowers we pasted onto cards together now sit on my bedroom shelf, like the many words she

20   shared with me sit in my memory. Often, at night, the words play over and over again in those silent spaces of my mind that speak to me when I am very still.

When my grandmother died, I remember promising myself, *I'm going to put her words down, just*

25   *as I remember them, in a story. And I will try to make that story as good as it can be.*